Ode to a Master

DOUGLAS BUTLER

PUBLISHED BY FIDELI PUBLISHING INC.

ISBN: 978-1-60414-952-4

Ode to a Master

DOUGLAS BUTLER

PUBLISHED BY FIDELI PUBLISHING INC.

ISBN: 978-1-60414-952-4

Ode to a Master

I shall be telling this with a sigh
Somewhere ages and ages hence
Two roads diverged in a wood and I —
I took the one less traveled by,
And that has made all the difference.

— Robert Frost, "The Road Not Taken"

Michael Milkovich is ninety-seven. As he wends his way to the century mark, one solitary voice must say that he was much more than a successful coach known for his wrestling clinics and a conqueror of the wrestling world. In short order, he was also an astute businessman, an expert fisherman, and an intelligent teacher of industrial arts (with a Master's degree) and of driver's education.

As well, he was a woodworker who could build anything (including a baseball field in his backyard — if you build it, they will come), a stock market maven, a good family man, an acceptable guitar player and singer, and an author on the subject of wrestling. He even dabbled in psychology.

I want to emphasize what a good teacher he was, although this is not unusual with wrestling coaches. Coach Milkovich had three salient qualities: excellent *judgment*, *intelligence*, and *creativity*. These qualities served him well beyond coaching and into the classroom, where he excelled.

His coaching prowess was evident early. In November 1956, *The Ohio High School Athlete* placed two masters on its cover: Jack Nicklaus on the front, prior to winning six Masters golf tournaments, and Mike Milkovich on the back, prior to coaching ten state wrestling titles. How did the editors of that magazine know what greatness lay in store for these two men?

Milkovich's Champions

M ike Milkovich coached everyone to championships — brothers, nephews, sons, and even himself. All were state champions. And some of the prominent wrestlers he coached became excellent coaches themselves.

John Borszcz coached his community college to a national championship; Frank Romano coached his college, Notre Dame, to a national championship; Mike's son, Pat Milkovich, led his wrestling club to a national championship.

One prominent wrestler coached by Mike Milkovich was Joe Peritore, a two-time state champion and two-time national finalist. Peritore made the Lehigh Hall of Fame (a three-time All-American), received a Master's degree from the Harvard School of Business, and became a Fortune Top 50 executive.

Champions are made when ordinary people do extraordinary things.

—Jim Valvano,
coach of North Carolina State 1983 NCAA basketball national champions

Still I believe that Coach Milkovich did his most amazing coaching when he took underdogs to championships. The first was John Borszcz, who had *two* state champions in his weight. Only his coach believed that he would win the state title, but there was John pinning the previous state champion to claim the title. An unforgettable victory.

Another was Gary Sorace. He did not make the varsity team until late in his senior year. He met the returning state champion in the regional tournament and was handily beaten. Gary met that same wrestler in the finals of the state tournament.

Once again, nobody gave Gary a chance, but his coach did. After a slow start in the first period, Gary soundly beat the state champion. Milkovich coached other underdogs to success too; Conrad Calendar, for one, completely dominated an opponent in the state finals after losing to him a week earlier. How was this possible?

It is my belief that Michael Milkovich was one of the few coaches who used his own willpower to help his athletes win. His influence was comparable to that of another, more famous coach, Iowa wrestling coach Dan Gable. Not only did Gable affect the athletes he coached, but also the fellow members of his own team — the 1972 American Olympic team.

Dan pulled several medal winners of that team onto the podium through his rigorous training program. His willpower, along with his personality, was so strong that he influenced anyone with whom he had contact —

including the opposition. Milkovich was much the same way and *attained results another coach could not even imagine.* Coach Milkovich did it all the time, but he would have said that a winner never quits, and as a coach he would never quit on one of his athletes.

Michael Milkovich was brilliant at recognizing other people's good ideas and incorporating them into his own program. Therein lies the famous story of his trip to Greenville, Pennsylvania. In the 1960's, there were about 10,000 people living in this small manufacturing city.

The city, about 80 miles from Cleveland, Ohio, was on the Shenango River, and may be best known for its proximity to Thiel College, and for being the home of Stefan Banic, the inventor of the parachute. It was also the home of the *Trojans*, one of the finest high school wrestling teams in Pennsylvania. Eventually the school had 10 state champions to its credit — Coach Milkovich *knew* he had to pay them a visit. They had to be doing something right, didn't they?

During the 1960's, travel of a high school sports team was somewhat limited, but that did not stop the Coach. He arranged a bus trip from Ohio to Pennsylvania to scrimmage the outstanding Greenville team with the always tough Maple Heights team. Everything turned out as expected except for one thing: Greenville had one takedown that absolutely destroyed the Maple Heights team — the feared "*shuck*" move.

Coach Milkovich was determined to have his team learn that maneuver and both teams practiced it to perfection in Greenville. The challenge of this wrestling move was a subtle nuance that one needed to perfect in order to master the takedown. "Hold the elbow tight and pull the arm down." Some wrestlers are uniquely suited for certain maneuvers and cannot be stopped once everything is learned. The question is always, who are the best candidates and can they master it?

The bus left Greenville for Maple Heights, but Coach Milkovich was not finished. After the journey home, Mike Milkovich directed the bus to the Maple Heights High School, retrieved the wet training gear, and practiced the shuck, again, so it would not be forgotten. (Now the takedown was completely imbedded in the wrestlers' mind, so it could be performed through instinct alone.)

The Coach could list numerous athletes from his team who used the shuck and won important matches because of it. There was a period of time before the rest of Ohio caught up with Coach Milkovich, but once they did, he had learned something new that again placed him above his peers. The state of Ohio was constantly making rule changes, but it was never enough to derail the Maple Heights juggernaut. They were simply superior.

Coach Milkovich has a *school named for him*, but it should be in recognition of his excellence as an educator as well as a coach. It is a shame that there are no audio records of him at Maple Heights High School because he had a distinctive and memorable voice.

When a wrestler became a state champion in Ohio, Mike Milkovich would call him Champ. You could walk down the halls of his school and hear him yell, *"Champ, champ,"* and it was the most beautiful sound anyone could hear. In the old days, wrestlers did not get much for winning a state championship, but hearing Mike Milkovich call someone "Champ" was worth it all — and they were all champs for life.

Well the first time I talked to him (Milkovich, Sr.) we spoke for over an hour. He was friendly, gracious, funny, and a man who pulled no punches. He never knew what "No Comment" was. I loved the man, and still do. He had a great program in part because he was the first coach to have a junior high feeder system into Maple Heights High School. He was Cleveland's original King, not LeBron James.

— Pat Galbincea,
The Cleveland Plain Dealer

Name that tune

Urban Meyer, the Ohio State football coach, is trying something new with his football team: introducing music as part of his practice sessions. Milkovich beat Urban to it by sixty years, having done it in the 1950s. This is just one example of the creativity both coaches have manifested while trying to bring their teams to the peak of competitiveness.

The favorite modality of Milkovich was the 1950s jukebox. He had another teacher (Jim Gates) come to the wrestling room and play, in order, *all* the records that were in the jukebox. Some of the songs were silly, like "How Much Is That Doggie in the Window?" (thank you, Patti Page, but really), and others had more meaning, such as the team favorite, *"Green Door."*

To digress, the big rival for the Mustangs of Maple Heights, Milkovich's team, was the Bedford Bearcats. As their name would imply, the Bedford wrestlers were tough and a bit scary. They would wear white bathrobes, and early on their fearsome coach was named — you guessed it — *Trojan.* The color of Bedford was green. The only one who was not afraid of green was Milkovich, who was not only the proud owner of green wrestling tights, but also could beat anyone on his team or any other team. (Bedford was later known for gentler things, such as Halle Berry becoming the school's prom queen.)

When "Green Door" came on the jukebox, bedlam erupted in the wrestling room. In a lesson in takedowns, a larger wrestler would escort a smaller hapless opponent onto the mat. If the opponent was standing, he would get taken down with a pancake. *Wham!*

If the opponent was on his knees, it was a snapdown. *Bam!* Remember, the mats in those days were made of hard canvas, not the soft rubber we have today. *Ouch!* All the while, we at Maple Heights worried about Bedford.

The music started with a clock ticking —

> *Midnight, one more night without sleepin'*
> *Watchin', till the morning comes creepin'*
> *Green door, what's that secret you're keepin'?*

It was best to memorize the order of the tunes on the jukebox and get the hell out of the wrestling room before "Green Door" came on. Wrestlers either needed their ankles taped or had to go to the bathroom — any excuse to make a quick exit.

> *Knocked once, tried to tell 'em I'd been there*
> *Door slammed, hospitality's thin there*
> *Wonder, just what's goin' on in there*

"Green Door" by **Bob Davie** and **Marvin Moore**

Bedford had a unique old gymnasium — it was small and oval, and you could view the wrestling match from the balcony. This perspective was entirely different when you saw the match from above, rather than from the side (much in the same way as when a track meet or a nine-man crew race is seen from above — in the latter, every surge of every boat is evident to the spectator).

Also, when a wrestling match is viewed from above, the spectator is very involved, becoming, in a sense, part of the event. There was many a match where it looked as if one of the spectators (probably me) was going to fly down from the Bedford balcony to join the fray on the mat. You had a choice of landing on the referee or the brute from Bedford.

Milkovich said that theater was good for the sport, but you have to admit that a fan flying down to join the match would have been more entertaining than anything professional wrestling could conjure up. Now the importance of the dual meet rivalry is disappearing from wrestling, and it makes you wish for the days of yore. *Ah Bedford, how I miss thee!*

Progeny

*My father gave me the greatest gift
anyone could give another person,
he believed in me.*

Jim Valvano,
coach of North Carolina State 1983 NCAA
basketball national champions

As a father, Michael Milkovich was party to one of the great dynasties in American sport history. He passed on some of his better qualities to each of his four sons and two daughters. Here are the four *hermanos*:

Michael Milkovich, Jr. was the eldest son and an excellent wrestler and coach. But he also had the great judgment of his father and won sport contests published in the magazine, *Amateur Wrestling News*. Michael was a state champion, an outstanding collegiate wrestler, and finally an assistant coach under his father. Michael was an All-American in 1970.

Dan Milkovich showed the intelligence and creativity of his father as the wrestling coach at Cuyahoga Heights High School. The school, known for academics, presented quite a challenge to him, an athletic coach. But Dan, like his father, was like an extra weapon on the wrestler's hip — when he was in the coach's corner.

How good a coach was he? He originally inherited a team of a meager six wrestlers and molded them into a championship caliber team. In 2005, Dan was chosen Coach of the Year in his division for the state of Ohio. He was also an accomplished wrestler in high school and in college.

Tom Milkovich was one of the greatest wrestlers from the state of Ohio. He had his father's competitiveness, as well as his good judgment. Tom almost never made a mistake, but his career had always been marked by "what-ifs?" What if Tom hadn't been injured in college — how good would he have been? What if Auburn had given Tom a fair chance to coach that team —how far could he have taken them? Could a Southern team be a force in wrestling? We will never know.

Tom was a three-time state champion, and a four-time undefeated Big Ten champion. He was a collegiate national champion and beat the wrestler (twice) who interrupted Dan Gable's unblemished collegiate record. He also won the Midlands twice, and was an All-American.

Pat Milkovich, named after the formidable wrestler Pat Palumbo, was one of the most intelligent wrestlers to ever step on the mat. The word *"finesse"* epitomizes his style. He was named Michigan State's Greatest Wrestler.

I feel he should be a candidate for the *Sportsmanship Award*. Here are some other renown candidates: Jack Nicklaus in golf, a Payne Stewart Award winner, (Gary Player said that Jack was humble in victory and gracious in defeat); John Havlicek in basketball, (as good an athlete as he was, with eight NBA titles, his family said he was an even better father); and Brooks Robinson in baseball, a Roberto Clemente Award winner, (the author of Brooks's biography, Doug Wilson, was criticized for only saying nice things about Brooks. Doug's answer: all you can say is nice things about Brooks). And, of course, there were the incomparable Wayne Gretzky in hockey (a Lady Byng Memorial Trophy 5-time winner), Jackie Robinson in baseball, and Roger Federer in tennis, (a winner of the Stephen Edberg Sportsmanship Award, 11 times and counting).

We must also recognize all the winners (too numerous to mention) of the Sportsmanship Award for the NFL and the NBA, named in honor of Art Rooney, Sr. and Joe Dumars, respectively. Baseball has, since 1971, given the Roberto Clemente Award, which honors sportsmanship in its sport (too late for Lou Gehrig and Stan Musial, who incidentally won the *Sports Illustrated* sportsperson of the year in 1957).

Golf has, since 2000, given the Payne Stewart Award for sportsmanship. Hockey to its credit has, since 1924, recognized sportsmanship by giving the Lady Byng Memorial Trophy to a deserving player.

Let's look at the incident that made Pat rank with the greatest. In 1975, Pat was wrestling for his third NCAA title. The tournament was held in Princeton, New Jersey, and his opponent was John Fritz from Penn State (who later became the coach there).

Now John was a very slick wrestler and his signature move was a "*duck under*" takedown. The fans at Princeton saw that move all tournament long, and John was so good that the maneuver looked more like something from a gymnastic routine rather than wrestling. When John pulled it on Pat Milkovich, the crowd made a whooshing sound that reverberated throughout the arena.

But now it was Pat's turn. He took John down with a "*shuck*" that looked more like a judo move. Pat moved his opponent to the side, then used his opponent's own strength to complete the takedown. The fans went wild; those two wrestlers put on a veritable clinic, which even extended into the overtime period.

Eventually, John Fritz won the match, but Pat exhibited the ultimate in *sportsmanship*: he stood in the center of the mat and *applauded* the winner. No one who saw it will ever forget the gesture of the former two-time champion (who lost) toward his rival (who won).

In the movie *Foxcatcher*, Mrs. du Pont tells her son that wrestling is a "low" sport — a dirty and sweaty sport, one that might hurt the opponent, as opposed to an elite sport (like crew). But certainly Pat Milkovich dispelled that low image by raising his sport to the highest ethical level of amateur athletics. (Note that in nine-man crew, the winners garner the shirts from the backs of the losing team, but I guess that's fair because it is a tradition.)

Pat was also *gracious to other opponents* who beat him, praising their athletic abilities and character to the press. Pat was a high school champion in Ohio, a two-time national champion while at Michigan State, and a four-time national finalist. He was the youngest athlete to win a NCAA wrestling championship, a four-time All-American, and was inducted into the National Wrestling Hall of Fame in 2000.

> *The most important career decision you are going to make is whether or not you have a life partner, and who that life partner is.*
>
> **Sheryl Sandberg,**
> Operating Officer of Facebook

Time out — *time out!* When it comes to progeny, we have only talked about one-half of the equation. As exemplary a father-coach as Milkovich was, he could not put into his offspring what God left out. The children inherited the DNA of both their father, the coach, and their mother, Barbara. (Mike once said that he had to work very hard to catch that redhead.) What a superb choice.

In the early days of Maple Heights wrestling, after the match was over, Coach Milkovich would bring out the four *hermanos*, who were quite young at the time, to give the crowd an exhibition in wrestling. What fun! It was one of the few times you could meet Barbara. I can only say that to meet her was to love her — she was not just ravishing, but she was smart and possessed an uncanny sense of intuition.

Am I right,
or am I right?

*"Don't let the noise of others' opinions
drown out your own inner voice."*
— **Steve Jobs**

So people who are *sure of themselves* seem to possess several qualities: they have no doubts, they do not hesitate to act quickly, and they do not let others influence their actions. Mike Milkovich Sr. had self-assurance, in spades.

It was never more evident than at the 1966 state wrestling tournament, from the St. John Arena, on the Ohio State University campus. Mike Milkovich Jr. was wrestling for the 112-pound championship, and his father (because he was also his coach) was seated at the end of his son's mat.

Part way through the match, Mike Jr. was apparently in jeopardy, and 10,000 fans rose to their feet to see the coach's son get pinned. (Because both father and son were from Maple Heights, they had to endure the wrath of most of those fans at the arena. The ethos was that if Maple Heights never won again, it would be *too soon*).

Coach Milkovich then sprang to his feet and lay down on the floor at the mat's edge to see how much trouble his son was having. He came to the conclusion that his son was not in any trouble at all. Still the raucous crowd was screaming for a Milkovich to lose.

Then the Coach did an amazing thing — he sat back in his chair, stretched his feet out and put his hands behind his head. This gesture told all the fans that no matter what they thought was happening, the Coach knew otherwise — and, of course, he was right. No points were awarded to the Maple Heights opponent, and Mike Jr. went on to win the state championship.

Still the most defining event of the evening did not occur until the medal ceremony for the 112-pound contestants. Normally, these ceremonies are rather dull, with each wrestler getting his medal placed around his neck, followed by perfunctory applause from the fans.

This ceremony was running to form, until the fourth place winner (Charles Bartee) received his medal. Now Charles' appearance was quite like that of any normal wrestler, although he did have particularly large hands.

When Charles was on the podium, 10,000 fans rose to their feet. First they started to cheer, then they stomped their feet, and then they gave some shrill whistles, and finally above all of this noise you could hear them call out his name, "Charles." It was a cacophony of sound that was indescribable, much in the same way the rebel yell was heard in the Civil War.

Still it was not over, the sound became louder, similar to a musical crescendo. The cheering continued past three minutes and approached five minutes. Charles began to cry on the podium, as this ovation was never-ending.

Why the standing ovation for this athlete? After all, he lost two matches and apparently did not do anything special. Coach Milkovich was also on his feet, acknowledging this boy's achievement. Charles was a credit to the sport of wrestling, which has always been the fairest of sports (as long as you make the weight).

What *everyone* knew who was present at the state final was that Charles *did* achieve something special, because he was — *blind.*

> *"He can take his'n and beat your'n,*
> *then take your'n and beat his'n."*
>
> **Bum Phillips,**
> football coach, Houston Oilers

After Michael Milkovich Sr. won his second state team championship in 1957, the coach had a message to all wrestlers in Cleveland. *"Hear ye, hear ye,"* all wresters in the Cleveland area were invited to work out with the Maple Heights wrestlers to avail themselves of the team's superior system and facilities.

Who would have the nerve to take up on the coach's offer? There was a wrestler (John Wolter) from nearby

Cleveland Heights, who wanted to give it a go because he said, "There are no competitive heavyweights available at my school."

So John toodled over daily to Maple Heights to get the training he wanted. And besides, Maple Heights had a very good heavyweight in Jack Beechuk, and a prior state champion wrestler at the weight below heavyweight, who would come to Maple Heights just to work out.

How did it go? Well, John Wolter was undefeated and was well on his way to a state championship. Only one person stood in his way, the heavyweight wrestler from Maple Heights! The two met in the semifinals of the state championship in a hotly fought match. You can imagine that the Maple Heights fans were having apoplexy because Wolter had trained at their school.

The anxiety of the fans only turned to horror as Wolter forged an early lead. Why did the coach let him train at Maple Heights? *Woe is me!* Ah, but you must always have faith in the coach's judgment.

Jack Beechuk took it to John Wolter later in the match, won the bout easily, and later won the state championship — (while John Wolter placed third). In the end, the only match John lost was to Maple Heights — so much for the superior system and facility.

What Maple Heights really had was Mike Milkovich, who could beat you with one hand tied behind his back. What Michael Milkovich showed, time and time again, was that he had incredible intelligence and judgment.

The coach's nephew, Jamie Milkovich, had the right idea — if you want to be the best you had to be part of the best. Jamie Milkovich won his state championship with his uncle as his coach, the man who always wore a red shirt for his athletes. Jamie had made a good choice.

Legacy

Milkovich v. Lorain Journal Co.

Good name in man and woman, dear my lord
Is the immediate jewel of their souls.
But he that filches from me my good name
Robs me of that which not enriches him,
And makes me poor indeed.
William Shakespeare
Othello

In 1974, Milkovich and his team, the Maple Heights Mustangs, were involved in an altercation at a match with another team, the Mentor Cardinals. Both Milkovich and the superintendent of his school system testified in a hearing before the Ohio High School Athletic Association, which resulted in the team being placed on probation. That same year, they testified again during a suit brought by several parents, in which a county court overturned the ruling of the Athletic Association, allowing the team to again compete.

In 1975, the day after the court's decision, the *News-Herald* of Willoughby, Ohio, (owned by the Lorain Journal Company) published a column, "Maple Beat the Law With the 'Big Lie,'" by Mr. J. Theodore Diadiun, which claimed that Milkovich lied under oath (a felony under Ohio law).

Milkovich sued Diadiun and his newspaper for libel. (It was questionable whether the reporter was even at the athletic event.) But could a columnist's opinion be considered libelous? The ensuing legal case, which spanned almost *fifteen years* including appeals, rolled through the Ohio judicial system.

It was twice denied a United States Supreme Court appeal; only years later did the Supreme Court finally decide to hear the case. Milkovich — who had battled the respondent Lorain Journal Company, the ACLU, the Dow Jones, the *New York Times* and the *Washington Post,* all of which stood behind Diadiun and the *News-Herald* — won the First Amendment case in an astounding 7 to 2 decision in 1990.

Chief Justice of the United States Supreme Court, William Rehnquist, called the *Milkovich* case an "odyssey of litigation." There are numerous reasons for this description, many of which rest with the legal team Milkovich assembled to pursue this litigation. First, was the coach himself, who fought to his last penny to preserve his reputation and his dignity.

Second, was the attorney who represented Michael Milkovich before the Supreme Court, Brent L. English, who stated, "There is also a need for an individual to be able to recover for reputational damage." Mr. English donated at least $250,000 worth of his time for this case.

And finally, there was a second attorney in the legal team, John D. Brown. John's story is interesting because he had been a member of the Maple Heights wrestling team, as were his older brother Jim, and his younger brother Bob.

There was no quit in that legal team, which is why they prevailed against the media giants in the end. To put the result in simple terms, *Don't take on Mike Milkovich* unless you are ready for the match of your life, and that match might include overtime.

What will history remember most about Michael Milkovich and why? In many ways, his coaching career will be tangential to what he should be most remembered for: *Milkovich v. Lorain Journal Co.* We cannot overemphasize the magnitude of the victory of this **one man**. Let's look at some significant facts related to this case:

1. It is a *First Amendment case* involving the issue of free speech and freedom of the press.

2. Legal precedents were the *New York Times Co. v. Sullivan* and *Gertz v. Robert Welch, Inc.*, which clarified and expanded what could be said in the press without fear of litigation.

3. The *New York Times* and the *Washington Post* were fresh from their own Supreme Court victory concerning the Pentagon Papers, then published by both newspapers.

Michael Milkovich met all challenges in the Ohio courts, but the Supreme Court of the United States was conservative in nature and apt to follow the legal precedents of the *New York Times Co. v. Sullivan* and *Gertz v. Robert Welch*, which wouldn't have worked in Milkovich's favor.

Also, the *New York Times* and *Washington Post* filed *amicus* (friend of the court) *briefs* for the *Lorain Journal Co.*, and the opposition (the newspaper) had deeper pockets for legal expenses.

It clearly was David (Milkovich) versus three Goliaths (the *Lorain Journal Company*, the *New York Times*, and the *Washington Post*). And the winner was Milkovich, in an absolutely stunning victory, even without the use of his slingshot. Go figure!

To this day, law reviews are discussing *Milkovich v. Lorain Journal Co.*; the case remains alive and vibrant, as it is debated now and will be for decades to come. State legislatures are passing laws to clarify the case and state bars are using it as part of their examinations.

This brings me to a personal anecdote that shows how some Supreme Court cases can impact the lives of Americans far beyond what you would expect. So it was for me after the *Milkovich* case was decided.

Two law students, who were patients in my medical practice, were studying for the Maryland Bar Exam. They would come to my office with their laptops in tow, totally focused on the impending bar exam and incapable of relating anything to me about their medical conditions.

Since they did not want to discuss medicine with me, I decided to talk law with them: the *Milkovich* case with all its various twists and turns. Much to my amazement, the students had never heard of this case, not in their law school nor in their bar review course.

"What do you know about the *Milkovich* case?" I asked.

Silence!

"It involves First Amendment law. Are you interested?"

Most definitely, was the response. We proceeded to discuss the *Sullivan* and the *Gertz* cases, as distinguished from the *Milkovich* case. After two visits to my office, the subject was never mentioned again. I fully expected to never address it again, nor, after discharging the patients, did I expect to hear from my two patients, either. I was wrong.

Several weeks later, I received a phone call from one of my patients who had just finished the Maryland Bar Exam. He excitedly told me that the very first question — an essay — in the constitutional law section, concerned the facts (without mentioning the name of the case) of the *Milkovich* case. My patient remembered all the particulars from our discussion and "smoked" that question.

After that section of the bar exam was completed, he met other students who took the exam. "What was that first question on the constitutional law section?" asked the other students. No one recognized the *Milkovich* case except one other student, who happened to be my other patient. Both patients passed the bar and thanked me profusely for the discussions in my office.

I never told them that the *Milkovich* case was the only case I knew about in any great depth, and it was just a stroke of luck that it was such an important section on their bar exam. I had no precognition and had never had any other patients who had taken the bar exam.

Undoubtedly, Michael Milkovich would pick up his sword and fight once again, if, by a quirk of law, the case was reconsidered and overturned by another case at the Supreme Court. This fight would be led by a man in his tenth decade. Just talking with the coach left me with the impression that *I'd always want that man on my side*.

The final action by Michael Milkovich was patently magnanimous:

> After the Supreme Court ruled against them, *The Journal Co.* reached an out-of-court settlement with Mr. Milkovich, who had retired. Mr. Milkovich and Mr. Diadiun (reporter for the newspaper) have since mended their ways and appeared together for discussions of this case and the First Amendment law it represented. Mr. Diadiun is now employed by the *Cleveland Plain Dealer*.

I don't think there is any question that winning this case was the greatest victory of his career.

Conclusion

When Michael Milkovich, Jr. won his state championship, his father told him, "Michael, as good as you are, your younger brothers are going to be even better."

I would hasten to add that *no one* would be better than the father. Michael Milkovich, Sr. was an Ohio state wrestling champion in 1941, the National Wrestling Coach of the Year in 1976, and was inducted into the National Wrestling Hall of Fame in 1983.

Then, of course, he became the improbable victor in his Supreme Court case in 1990.

As Franklin Delano Roosevelt said, referring to other men of the World War Two generation: this man, part of the greatest generation, had *a rendezvous with destiny*.

> *It matters not how strait the gate,*
> *How charged with punishments the scroll,*
> *I am the master of my fate,*
> *I am the captain of my soul.*
>
> **William Ernest Henley,** "Invictus"

Further Reading about *Milkovich v. Lorain Journal Co.*

- **Statements of Opinion Can Be Libelous, Court Rules:**
  (http://www.washingtonpost.com/archive/politics/1990/06/22/statements-of-opinion-can-be-libelous-court-rules/03e4036e-b1d5-4580-adc4-c95a2d21d39f/)

- *Milkovich v. Lorain Journal Co.*
  (https://www.law.cornell.edu/supremecourt/text/497/1)

- **Milkovich Revisited: "Saving the Opinion Privilege**
  (http://scholarship.law.duke.edu/cgi/viewcontent.cgi?article=3170&context=dlj)

- **LAW; How a '74 Fracas Led to a High Court Libel Case**
  (http://www.nytimes.com/1990/04/20/us/law-how-a-74-fracas-led-to-a-high-court-libel-case.html?pagewanted=all)

See also: *Mustang* by Jim Kalin, Shem Creek Press, Los Angeles, 2016.

About the Author

Douglas Butler attended Ohio State University, University of California-Berkeley, Case Western Reserve University-School of Medicine and Case Western Reserve University-School of Law.

He was a member of the department of surgery at Carroll Hospital Center and is a member of the American College of Legal Medicine.

Appointments: Catholic Medical Missionary — Ecuador.

His heroes include Nancy Writebol, medical missionary; Dr. Kent Brantly, medical missionary; and David F. Walbert, attorney.

He is both a doctor and a lawyer in Maryland, where he presently lives.

CPSIA information can be obtained
at www.ICGtesting.com
Printed in the USA
BVOW03s0330070917
494082BV00001B/2/P